On Phillips Creek

poems by

Natalie Kimbell

Finishing Line Press
Georgetown, Kentucky

I believe that one can never leave home.
Maya Angelou, Letter to My Daughter

On Phillips Creek

This book is dedicated to all who believed in me as a writer before I believed in myself, especially my children, Nathan and Tricia.

Copyright © 2024 by Natalie Kimbell
ISBN 979-8-88838-626-2 First Edition
All rights reserved under International and Pan-American Copyright Conventions. No part of this book may be reproduced in any manner whatsoever without written permission from the publisher, except in the case of brief quotations embodied in critical articles and reviews.

ACKNOWLEDGMENTS

With much thanks, I wish to acknowledge the following publications where my work originally appeared, sometimes in slightly different forms:

"River," as "I Am a River of Stories," in *Women Speak*
"The Book of the Dead," in *The Anthology of Appalachian Writers-Dorothy Allison Version*
"Leaf Burning," as "Leaf Spinning," in *American Diversity Report*
"On the Pound Near Phillips Creek," in *Pine Mountain Sand and Gravel-Appalachia Unmasked*
"At the Donut Shop," in *Garfield Lake Review*
"In Retrospect," originally under the title "You," in *Chattanooga Writers' Anthology*
"To My Last Lovers at the Knoxville Body Farm," and "Awe in March," in *Chattanooga Writers' Anthology*
"On Rainy Days," and "Hope Made Simple," in *Monterey Poetry Review*
" Sheer Memory," "Strip Me Naked," "Kin Cursing," and "Why Did I Wish," in *Mildred Haun Review*
"Mourning the Death of My Ex-Husband's Second Wife," "When Your Wish is Granted," and "At the Catawba Sanitorium," in the *Anthology of Appalachian Writers-Barbara Kingsolver Version*

Publisher: Leah Huete de Maines
Editor: Christen Kincaid
Cover Art: Michelle Walling Collier
Author Photo: Beverly Key
Cover Design: Beto Cumming

Order online: www.finishinglinepress.com
  also available on amazon.com

Author inquiries and mail orders:
Finishing Line Press
PO Box 1626
Georgetown, Kentucky 40324
USA

Contents

The Spring

River 2
The Book of the Dead 3
Leaf Burning 4
For My Dad 6
Sheer Memory 7
Kin Cursing 8
At the Catawba Sanitorium 9
On the Pound Along Phillips Creek in Virginia 10
When Your Wish Is Granted 11

The Run-Off

Dawn Seduction 14
July Lullaby 15
Dandelion Fireworks 16
Awe in March 17
Waiting for Words 18

The Creek Bed

Strip Me Naked 20
Why Did I Wish? 21
The Gift 22
At the Donut Shop 23
On Rainy Days 24
In Retrospect 25
Mourning the Death of my Ex-Husband's Second Wife 26
To My Last Lovers at the Knoxville Body Farm 27
If Gratitude Were a Woman 28
Something Blue 29
Hope Made Simple 31

Introduction

My maternal grandmother, Oma Mullins Edwards, grew up on the Pound in a holler somewhere between Pound, Virginia, and Jenkins, Kentucky. The Mullins Homeplace, depicted on the cover, was the first home I came to after my birth at the Park Avenue Hospital in Norton, Virginia. Throughout my childhood and teen years from 1960 to the early1980's, we visited my grandmother for a week or two during the summer, dropping back in time living without plumbing, telephone, or television. Meals cooked on a wood stove, baths in basins, teeth brushed spitting off the back porch, and trips to the outhouse imprinted visceral memories. Phillips Creek ran a few hundred yards from the house. Many afternoons I sat in the swing on the front porch and listened to the rush of water. It's music and the cadence of voices accompany my work. Today, the house, the creek, and all the natural features, including the mountaintops no longer exist. All of it has been leveled by economics and the quest for coal. This book is a small tribute to that place and the heritage that flows within me.

The Spring

Time is a sort of river of passing events, and strong is its current; no sooner is a thing brought to sight than it is swept by and another takes its place, and this too will be swept away.

Marcus Aurelius

RIVER

I am a river of women's stories
        passing fluid, from mother to daughter—
distinct, like the sound of stones
        skimming across pools of eternity.

I am the collected voices of my women kin
        who rise above and below the flood line.
I am the keeper of salacious secrets
        and callous dispatches.

I carry stories, swept by time, flooded by grief
        of cousin Alifair whose husband didn't want a baby
forced to ride a horse until she aborted
        killing both her and the child.

I bear bold whispers between women about Silvanee,
        witch woman, my Grandma Oma said,
who wed my Uncle Irving, making him her bidder
        by lacing his drinks with a drop of herself.

I flow in rippling patterns
        repeating my Grandmother's,
my mother's, and my own history
        of loving men who would not stay.

I conjure back our women from the River Styx,
        resurrecting them in my breath,
raising them up out of shallows,
        making them current.

I am a river.

THE BOOK OF THE DEAD

*Dedicated to my granddaughter Denali
whose seven year-old-wisdom inspired this poem*

My granddaughter Denali calls it *The Book of the Dead*.
A brown photo album with ornate gold trim,
smelling like chenille bedspreads and musty rooms,
that opens with her grandfather, five greats removed.
Closes with a high school portrait of me.

It's not the Book of the Dead,
I tell her,
offering my colored image as proof.
I smile, and say,
Look, Denali. I'm not dead.

But Grandma, you are close.

Denali lugs the album, urging me to settle,
scooting like a shuttle, weaving her bottom back
and forth on the sofa. Black leather cushions exhale
as I sit, balancing the musty weight
of yellowed ages on our mismatched thighs.

Denali folds the cover back in my hands.
With her fingers, she outlines the face
of Rueben Columbus Camp
frozen in tintype 100 years before she was born.

Again she retraces his face
as if to feel his cheek
through the magnetic veil,
then dabs her eyes with the same fingertips.

He doesn't know me.

She sighs, leans close,
makes me promise:
Grandma, when you die, tell the family my name.
Grandma, tell them, I'm coming.

LEAF BURNING

Leaf tornadoes whirl in funnels
shuffling fronds like playing cards.

Ragged edges tumble
into scattered mosaic shards.

Let nature mulch, for goodness' sake—
it's fun to let them dance

but Momma wants the whole yard raked,
says all those leaves will kill the grass.

Begrudgingly, I scrape dead leaves,
stack leaf-fall for a pyre.

But I want to do as I please
and dive in the leafy mire

and thrash among the waves,
fling myself into the leaf swell,

but Momma sets it all ablaze,
casting yet another spell.

Hypnotized by crack and sizzle,
rapt by irisated blaze,

I embrace the gray baptismal
with acrid tendrils of thick haze.

I stir the bewitching bier,
flinging ashes like fairy dust

unconscious of spreading fire
until I hear my Momma fuss.

She grabs my rake. Shames my fancy.
It's a wonder your head's not lost.

Smoke hovers and spreads
glazing grass like morning frost.

FOR MY DAD

for Jerome "Jerry" Jenkins

He grew up in a minefield
crisscrossed with serrated words,

Why couldn't it have been you instead of Sonny.

He, the imperfect son. Left-handed in a right-handed
society perpetually compared to a dead sibling?

By nineteen, already wearing a rap sheet like a medal,
he became an errant sailor, tattooed for Rosie, married to Pat,

a jail breaker, drug dealer, thief, brawler, my father,
handsome like Elvis with a Massachusetts brogue.

A grammar school dropout who sketched dyslexic poetry
on napkins. Made me follow rules he would break.

He told me, *To live free on the planet* .

He said, *Kid, never let them see you smile.*

On his birthday, we laid him in state with the grateful dead
looking now more like Jerry Garcia than Elvis.

Flaunted in his Last Chance Motorcycle Club colors,
a joint in his pocket and "Dirty Deeds Done Dirt Cheap"
                    reverberating in the vestibule.

SHEER MEMORY

Wind stirred white curtains,
fluttering translucent sheers,
like sunbaked sheets Momma hung,
when I was five or maybe six.

Fluttering translucent sheers,
dodging clean cotton in neat rows,
when I was five or maybe six,
billowing material snapping dry.

Dodging clean cotton in neat rows,
smelling linen pinched on the line,
billowing material snapping dry,
full sails rippling September clouds.

Smelling linen pinched on the line,
wind stirred white curtains,
full sails rippling September clouds.
like sunbaked sheets Momma hung.

KIN CURSING

Third cousin Doris sits legs-crossed,
scalding eyes interrupted only by smoke.
Two gnarled fingers clenched in a victory sign,
a hand swirling gin in cut crystal.

She draws on unfiltered Camels,
flips her hand back like hair,
right elbow close to her ribs.

She flicks embers in an emerald ashtray,
grinds the butt down. She lights another.

High cheekbones, gaunt body, thin lips,
she cocks her contempt with a tilt of her chin.
Raises hell high with *fuck this,* and *goddamn that*,
singes the air already hot from spew of kin-cursing.

Momma said cousin Doris left the mountains,
worked for NASA,
married well,
birthed two children. They left her.

She returned, reigned like a monarch over our mountains,
flaunted success and education against our poverty.

In the early morning hours, drunk, Doris would call Momma,
reminisce their adolescent companionship
until her two-in-the-morning, gin-filled rants
became crying jags or venomous belittling of my mother.

Momma coddled her, tried to make sense,
took the abuse of Doris's early morning tirades
until one evening Momma stopped,
took the phone off the cradle.

AT THE CATAWBA SANITORIUM

To Oma Edwards

They placed her in an iron lung,
a last resort to life.
She birthed daughters, never a son.
Young mother and wife

now death close, seventy pounds of flesh,
gasping air without conscious hope,
without time, exhausted of cash.
Her family trying to cope

in a tuberculosis nation.
Doctors searching for a cure.
Her sisters fought hesitation
and paid for a drug to help her endure.

Streptomycin, just a chance then, required cash
ninety dollars, a fortune during forty-seven.
but her sisters pulled together a cache,
the money was paid, the serum was given,

and from the dead, health rebounded.
The drug, an answer to many a prayer,
saved my grandmother from an early death,
saved many others from dying there.

She lived for over eighty years.
Lived to see grandchildren play.
She never forgot Catawba's nurses
or the debt she could never repay.

ON THE POUND ALONG PHILLIPS CREEKS IN VIRGINIA

The mold of earth and time threaded air,
disturbed only by sooty smoke and crack
of coal burning. The fireplace hissed, popped.
Ghost shadows licked walls and dark ceilings.

But I, hypnotized by voices in hushed tones,
edged on, wanting to be a part of them, comradery
of women after work stops. The music of mothers
whispering on the Pound on Phillips Creek.

Closer I drew, but out of sight, I huddled
nightgown over my knees in the darkened
hall between the pie safe and kitchen.
Pressed against the paneled wall,

I nestled there chilling on the floor, listening
to names muted in turbulence. Grandmother spoke
her brother's name, who passed the winter before.
Her speech heated, unleashed on his ex-wife, Silvanee.

*Why, she witched him! His money
was what she wanted. She caught her cum and laced
his drink. No man can resist the wilds of a witch.*
And with a spit, thrown words lodged inside my head.

Fifteen years later, as a teacher of teens,
I blushed when explosive words were thrown
between girls in a bombardment of sexual slurs,
when one spun the centrifuge of memory.

In an instant, with chilled understanding,
I huddled again in damp air and coal smoke
listening to the words from the mouths of mothers
along the banks of Phillips Creek on the Pound in Virginia.

WHEN YOUR WISH IS GRANTED

To the Mullins/Edwards home place

I last saw the homeplace in 1977,
in the holler near Pound, Virginia,
bordered by Phillips Creek
not far from Jenkins, Kentucky.

Then, dusty dump trucks rumbled
chiseled coal off nearby mountains.

I was seventeen and had no desire to remain.

Grandma stayed to protect the farm,
for as long as she dwelled on the land,
the children of her brothers and sisters
couldn't sell the ground to a stranger.

She became too feeble to stay
with no phone, no running water, no neighbors,
and great aunts and uncles sold the property to coal developers,
letting strangers plow circles deep into the homeplace,
leveling it until it was scraped of what we knew.

Someone took the cast iron stove,
another pulled off the cedar panels
that lined the room on the porch.
Someone else stripped fireplace mantels and hearthstones.
Coal developers plowed down the apple orchard and buried
the sweet spring, scattered the stacked stone foundation.

I'm not sure about the bodies marked by rocks
on the hillside. Soldiers was what Grandma believed,
their bodies part of a forgotten past.

Years late, we cousins went home to search the landscape,
took our mothers to locate the farm, violated laws to get close.
But the landmarks were leveled, the creek altered, the mountains
                                                                                         ground down.

Home exists now in photographs, in story,
in acrylic paint drawings on the bottom of an enamel wash pan
that I washed my hands in as a child
when I wished I was anyplace,
                                        but there.

The Run-Off

For life and death are one, even as the river and the sea are one.

Khalil Gibran

DAWN SEDUCTION

Dawn with her oh, so, slow, lifting skirt,
suggests Night do more than tease or flirt.
Forgo your gloomy cloak. Don't resist.
She leans in and offers him a tryst,
unbuttoning his black thinning shade,
exposing his pallor, she cascades
pastel lipstick hues all down his chest
(a ritual Night cannot resist).
Then, Dawn spreads across his spacious bed
offering her purples and her reds,
and Night blends shedding his mourning by
yielding honeysuckle-colored sky.
Dawn finishes him with arching ease.
The bold wood thrush cues dark Night's release.

JULY LULLABY

Clover heads gather sun's last rays in tree-lined meadows
stretching thin, gangly necks past chain-linked shadows.

Their teasing green and purple blossoms entice straggling bees
whose drone waxes and wanes in cadence with the easy breeze.

And diminishing honey-butter shafts yawn and fade
through a layered, canopied colander of leaf brocade,

while gnats upward whirl in caramel-coated spiraling arcs
and spiders ride silken comets ablaze with day's last sparks.

DANDELION FIREWORKS

fountains burst
stretch and sizzle
whistle-lit sparks
like spores skid air

dandelions disperse
seeds with silver
weeping like willows
against satin black sky

AWE IN MARCH

Midday fire winks on spider's silk
while a million fuses blaze overhead
where glinting sparks scatter against gray bark.

Glittered gossamer like a cobra writhes
while entombing dogwood blossoms and lilac clusters
in gauzy, twisted, breeze born balloons.

Pileated woodpeckers feast at dusk
rip silence from hollow echoes in dead elms
while spiders creep as shadows stroll.

Tree and bullfrog lull with their serenade
while dangled arachnids flutter on threads.
Colorless spider's lace trolls in darkness.

WAITING FOR WORDS

Metal gutters resonate
like a metronome marks time.
Slow raindrops reverberate,
weeds saturate and entwine.

Dawn's gray fog-spun cotton
weaves through variegated green
like thoughts almost forgotten,
subtle wisps like fairies preen.

Woodpeckers tap the dead trees,
search for some sustenance,
some energy to be seized.
Faith in their own endurance.

A rap, a penciled refrain.
A pause in my persistence.
I dip in the writer's vein
for gold in my resilience.

The Creek Bed

Time is the substance from which I am made. Time is a river which carries me along, but I am the river...

Jorge Luis Borges

STRIP ME NAKED

After Rhea Carmon

Strip me naked. See a generation from potted meat, poke sallet, hot lard poverty. The sawmill where my great-grandfather lost his fingers and gained a high board Company Bed for his trouble. See the depths of chiseled coal mines or the distress of birthing babies not expected to live—like my three-pound momma so tiny she had a shoebox bed. See my grandmother racked with tuberculosis clinging to iron lung air. Strip me naked. See my other great-parents as teens crossing from Naples to Ellis Island. See my blood on Normandy's beaches with Great Uncle Tommy Robbio. Strip me naked. Find outcasts downcast rising dragging depression, dyslexia, and deficiencies assumed to weaken sinews when struggle made them strong. This skin has birthed lawbreakers, policemen, drug dealers, homemakers, secretaries, drunkards, mechanics, teachers, counselors, military officers. Strip me naked. See my lovers, my fractures, my dreams. See words coursing in veins, documenting, protesting, celebrating, healing the past with the present, the living with the dead with such richness. Wish to wear this skin.

But it's mine.

WHY DID I WISH?

I glide into seventeen fast.
Put memory on like a dab of baby blue eyeshadow.
Hug my well-formed hips in soft denim
flaunt my long mahogany hair, whip
it like a great dark wave out the family's Caprice Classic.

So crisp a vision,
long after arthritis riddles
and hair thins gray,
long after mirrors reflect
bones cocooned
in withering mottled flesh.

At life's 6:00 p.m.
distant childhood tastes better.
Oranges at Christmas,
biscuits slathered in bacon gravy.
Age recalls the stiff spring
of my line-dried dress,
summons the awkward first kiss,
the speed of my lover's pulse—
a pulse that now only beats
on eternity's mounded hills.

Why did I wish for the fountain of age
as if I had countless dawns to squander—
endless petals to pull from a daisy's center?
How like a backward butterfly
I fluttered my finest first,
and end now encased in crepe skin.

THE GIFT

Exposed to the bone
a cat-clawed corpse sprawls
before the threshold,
newly wed to the doormat.

I turn toward the cat,
make a veiled threat,
watch him groom himself
from the whole affair.

I, too, divorce myself,
engage in ceremony,
bowing to what is raw
and ripped asunder.

And I take this gift
that doesn't look
like a gift,
and accept it as one.

AT THE DONUT SHOP

After Phyllis Koestenbaum

Basically, my body is a crème-filled donut. Something empty that must be filled. At the donut shop, they use crème-filled injectors to ejaculate into the holes. They are not gentle. They do not ask. I feel dirty eating the donut—the crème oozing on my fingers. I am empty. I want to feel full. I want not to think about being a donut. I hear a name that is not mine, but it is mine today. I am a color. I am a number. They give me a pill. They give me the opportunity to leave. I am a donut. Where will I go? I lay on the table. He puts my feet in stirrups. They are cold like me. He rakes what was growing. The scraping goes on. And on and on. They take what was inside, out. They arrange it on a tray. I think about dying. I am a donut who bleeds. Before I go to bed, I take more pills to sleep. I use a sanitary napkin to hold my blood. I stay awake.

I can't stop thinking about the horrible thing I saw on the news—about the children at the border. Little children taken away and placed in cages. Living, breathing children taken from families for months, for years, forever. My body embarrasses me, all blood and tears. When I am sick, I eat to feel better. Yesterday, I ate a bag of Twizzlers, a bag of circus peanuts, a bag of jelly beans, a bag of pork rinds. I don't worry. They are all fat-free. Free fat. I remember I am full.

I eat a donut.

ON RAINY DAYS

> *The purpose of art is washing the dust of daily life off our souls.*
> Pablo Picasso

        droplets splatter, like Monet's dotted jabs,
against rain-pelted window screens
blurring mundane multicolored outdoor furniture.

Upper empty panes offer lines of tree branches,
arching and bending unimpeded by mesh.
Suspended February oak leaves droop in saturated shapes,
resembling timepieces in Dali's *The Persistence of Memory*.

In spite, the clock tocks.
Hands point to unfolded laundry,
scattered correspondence, flaunted
dust, and flagrant dirty dishes.

From outside, a single sparrow's anthem pulls my ear,
squelching the tedious. I take my pen. Detail how
Monet beckons Warhol out of the bright yard-art chairs.

IN RETROSPECT

       I think you were watching me
even before I saw you
that night at the Chinese restaurant.
You observed me burying my purse
among my granddaughter's toys in the backseat.

And I'm almost positive that while I was dining
you drove a brick through my car window,
leaving a hailstorm of glass in her car seat,
stealing my purse containing my favorite
Clinique lipstick, a pack of Dentyne Ice,
a pair of Christmas earrings I had
haphazardly tossed in with the seventy-eight cents
I kept after a Walmart purchase.

And I realize you lifted my credit cards
and my checkbook and my DNA
from a well-licked KitKat wrapper.
But it took me time to realize
that you stole my trust.

And now I can't help anyone,
not even my granddaughter,
with Kleenex, or Germ-X, or Blistex.
I quit carrying a purse.
I carry paranoia and you.

MOURNING THE DEATH OF MY EX-HUSBAND'S SECOND WIFE

For Gwen

On the cusp of summer,
when my children requested I help their father
empty the house he'd shared with his second wife,
remove her possessions, donate them, or keep whatever we could use,

I squirmed in my gut
not wanting to scavenge,
but there was a good wool coat that fit me,
an unfinished bottle of Lancôme perfume
the children just wanted to throw away,
a brass lamp with a shade of dangling frippery,
a solid bedside table of unfinished wood
with decoupaged pastel flowers,
an emerald silk scarf that bore her fragrance,
a faded, cushioned wicker chair,
and three rattan stackable tables.

At first, I was startled by my own avarice,
but now so much of her rests in my home,
I think of her with warmth, believing
we could have been friends
and I mourn the loss of my ex-husband's second wife,
more than I mourn the loss of my marriage.

TO MY LAST LOVERS AT THE KNOXVILLE BODY FARM

The thought—
you will ponder my flesh
and even though I am silent,
I will speak to you and you will listen
answers some need in me.
Even without a pulse,
I remain an unexplored palace
through which questions will be answered,
gives me pleasure.

This is my last request for any passion,
the last time the physical me will be held.
This pacifies my fear of death,
that my body contributes to something,
that my body does not parade plastered
and pasted together before a parlor of people
waiting for dessert. That the last words said
over my body
will not be trite.

Lovers,
know whether you dress me up
and watch me decompose in silk, satin, cotton,
or clothe me not at all, I will still be yours.
Whether you dissect my eyes
or render my fat down to my bones,
I will be grateful
you made me feel desired
one last time.

IF GRATITUDE WERE A WOMAN

If Gratitude were a woman,
she'd wear a pearl-colored camisole
and silk panties with pale lace against her ample frame.
She would don oversized cotton t-shirts
and black leggings with leather ankle boots.

If Gratitude were a woman
she'd work with calloused hands,
and clean nails
her shoulders bent not in obeisance,
but in grace and tenacity like water.
Her scent, a dusting of lilac.
Her skin, the blush of summer peaches.

If Gratitude were a woman,
her words would not fawn
or be perfunctory,
but would well like unexpected tears,
her laughter light like the rippling
of a stream over creek pebbles.

If Gratitude were a woman,
she'd carry the aura of a star,
the hum of a kitten,
the bursting of a crocus through frozen dirt.

Above crisp white sheets,
she would stir
like the aroma of bold coffee
if Gratitude were a woman.

SOMETHING BLUE

The sun glistens on planters left
outside my February window,
unprepared for spring.
Dead and mangled vines
borrow time next to last summer's
Dollar Tree plastic pinwheels.

I watch as the wind sets
a yellowed holographic pinwheel
spinning kaleidoscopic shards
beyond brittle, once-red geraniums
to the flat glass.

With each spin
it grooms the branches back,
frees itself and sheds
old threads of once-fertile finery.

Another pot holds
a faded pinwheel of blue,
its petaled shapes married
to the skeleton of tomato vines
bound by the circle of a metal cage
unable to be ushered into new movement.

Motionless, like stiff characters on a wedding cake.

Something nags me to leave my room,
to set that pinwheel free.
An inner ache scolds
me to prepare the pots for rebirth.

I remember the smell of earth
and feel the tug of fertility,
but I am divorced
from the natural world by the pane.

On my side of the window,
I spend hours married to dead vows,
unwilling to let go of the July
when I bloomed into something blue
surrounded by golden sunflowers.

HOPE MADE SIMPLE

Drifting dandelion seeds, a wish midair,
soap bubbles tossed by a plastic wand,
afternoon sunlight in a prism of glass,
a smooth rock in the palm of my hand.

Yellow daffodils bursting though frozen chert,
vibrant spring color of fresh green grass,
French lilac scent through a window screen,
the ding of a soft-blown wind chime of brass.

Red cardinals posed in evergreens,
collected motley-hued autumn leaves,
the tingle of mouth-caught snowflakes,
pink buds on the twigs of wintered trees.

Spotting the twilight's first evening star,
the warmth of hot chocolate after snow,
words woven by endearing voices,
a seedling of corn starting to grow.

Multi-petaled wild roses lining the path,
resting on a sunny footbridge all alone,
the rush of Phillips Creek after a hard rain,
deep comfort in coming back home.

With Thanks

I wish to thank my Upper Cumberland Writers Project Honey Badgers, Sharon, Martha, Ashley, and Sara, who started and still support my writing adventure; to Darnell Arnoult, who made me say, I am a writer; to Aaron Smith, who made me dig deeper than was comfortable; to Connie Green and all the fellow writers in her Sweetwater classes, who made me believe in the possibility of my own chapbook; to the Thursday Night Ekphrastic Group for nurturing and making me write each week; to John C. Mannone, who edited and nudged this chapbook toward its final form and to Sue Dunlap, who gave life to this chapbook and to my spirit. To these supporters I give all the accolades a grateful heart can bestow.

Special thanks also to Sequatchie County High School students and colleagues who have surrounded me with warm celebration with each one of my individual publication successes.

Natalie Kimbell was born in Norton, Virginia, spent her early elementary school years in Worcester, Massachusetts, and then moved to Dunlap, Tennessee to find her home. She is a graduate of Sequatchie County High School and a graduate of the University of Tennessee at Chattanooga. She serves as an English and theater arts and creative writing instructor at her high school alma mater. This year, 2024, will mark her fortieth year as an educator.

Although writing most of her life, she only began releasing her writing in 2017. Since then, her work has placed in several contests and has appeared in publications such as the *Appalachian Writers Anthology, Women Speak, Pine Mountain Sand and Grave*l as well as in *The Mildred Haun Review and Tennessee Voices Anthology*. Though primarily a poet, Kimbell has also published creative nonfiction and ten-minute monologues.

www.ingramcontent.com/pod-product-compliance
Lightning Source LLC
Chambersburg PA
CBHW030051100426
42734CB00038B/1233